Cows Can't Quack

By Dave Reisman

Illustrations By Jason A. Maas

JumpingCowPress.com

JUMPING COW PRESS

For my parents,
Hilda & Arnie Reisman

Published by Jumping Cow Press
P.O. Box 2732
Briarcliff Manor, NY 10510

ISBN 13: 978-0-9801433-4-8
ISBN 10: 0-9801433-4-9

Sixth Paperback Edition
March 2019

Printed in China

1

Cows can't quack...

...but they can moo.

Moose can't moo...

4

...but they can grunt.

Goats can't grunt...

...but they can bleat.

Monkeys can't bleat.

...but they can chatter.

Kittens can't chatter...

...but they can meow.

Roosters can't meow...

...but they can
cock-a-doodle-do.

Crows can't
cock-a-doodle-do.

...but they can caw.

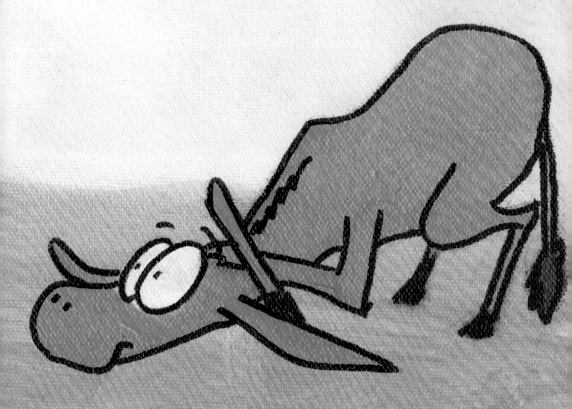

Donkeys can't caw...

...but they can hee-haw.

Frogs can't hee-haw...

18

...but they can croak.

Hippos can't croak...

...but they can bray.

Dolphins can't bray...

...but they can click.

Rabbits can't click...

...but they can coo.

Rhinos can't coo...

...but they can snort.

Wolves can't snort.

...but they can howl.

Geese can't howl...

...but they can cackle.

Whales can't cackle...

...but they can sing.

Penguins can't sing...

...but they can trumpet.

Hyenas can't trumpet...

...but they can laugh.

Eagles can't laugh...

...but they can scream.

39

Tigers can't scream...

...but they can roar.

Puppies can't roar...

...but they can snore.

44

Visit the Jumping Cow Press website for our shop, free printable learning resources and more!

www.jumpingcowpress.com

Available in Paperback, Stubby & Stout™ and eBook Formats